MYTHS ACROSS THE MAP

DRAGON MYTHS

Jenny Mason

Gareth Stevens Publishing

Please visit our website, **www.garethstevens.com**.
For a free color catalog of all our high-quality books,
call toll free 1-800-542-2595 or fax 1-877-542-2596.

CATALOGING-IN-PUBLICATION DATA

Names: Mason, Jenny.
Title: Dragon myths / Jenny Mason.
Description: New York : Gareth Stevens Publishing, 2018. | Series: Myths across the map | Includes index.
Identifiers: LCCN ISBN 9781538214411 (pbk.) | ISBN 9781538213681 (library bound) | ISBN 9781538214428 (6 pack)
Subjects: LCSH: Dragons--Juvenile literature. | Dragons--Folklore--Juvenile literature. | Animals, Mythical--Juvenile literature.
Classification: LCC GR830.D7 M37 2018 | DDC 398.24'54--dc23

Published in 2018 by
Gareth Stevens Publishing
111 East 14th Street, Suite 349
New York, NY 10003

Developed and Produced by Focus Strategic Communications, Inc.
Project Manager: Adrianna Edwards
Editor: Ron Edwards
Design and Composition: Ruth Dwight
Copy editors: Adrianna Edwards, Francine Geraci
Media Researchers: Adrianna Edwards, Paula Joiner, Maddi Nixon
Proofreader: Francine Geraci
Index: Ron Edwards, Maddi Nixon

Photo Credits: Credit Abbreviations: S Shutterstock; WC Wikimedia Commons. Position on the page: T: top, B: bottom, C: center, L: left, R: right.Cover, Title Page: adike/S; 4: Melkor3D/S; 5: Storozhenko/S; 6: Fotokostic/S; 7: releon8211/S; 8: Johan Swanepoel/S; 9 T: CHAINFOTO24/S, B: Lefteris Papaulakis/S; 10 L: reptiles4all/S, C: fotoslaz/S, R: David Thyberg/S; 11: thanongsak kongtong/S; 12: Zzvet/S; 13: Lauren Elisabeth/S; 14: Hiroki Ogawa/WC; 15: Brian Lasenby/S; 16: Nancy Bauer/S; 17: Elena11/S; 18: Theirislion/WC; 19: Mauvries/S; 20: somnuk jansinka/S; 21: SSSCCC/S; 22: jorisvo/S; 23: Image from The Fall of Princes, Public Domain/WC; 24: Melkor3D/S; 25: dovla982/S; 26: solarseven/S; 27: johannviloria/S; 28: Neirfy/S; 29: DM7/S; 30: feathercollector/S; 31: lev radin/S; 32: Vera Petruk/S; 33: Lefteris Papaulakis/S; 34: Flicker API/WC: OPIS Zagreb/S; 36: BelayaMedvedica/S; 37: Michael Rosskothen/S; 38: Josef Hanus/S; 39 L: imagewriter/S, R: Jastrow, Joseph. "The Mind's Eye." The Popular Science Monthly 54 (1898): 312. Internet Archive. Web. 16 May 2017; 40: Everett Historical/S; 41: Linda Bucklin/S, Background: Oleg1969/S; 42: Ammit Jack/S; 43: State Archives of Florida/Gaines; 44: Gisling/WC; 45: vectorEps/S; Design Elements: Margarita Miller/S, viewgene/S, yoshi0511/S.

Printed in the United States of America

CPSIA compliance information: Batch CW18GS: For further information contact
Gareth Stevens, New York, New York at 1-800-542-2595.

TABLE OF CONTENTS

WHAT IS A DRAGON? 4

ON A SCALE OF GOOD TO BAD 15

DRAGON BEHAVIOR 23

FIGHTING TOOTH AND CLAW 31

EVADING EXTINCTION 37

DRAGON MYTHS ACROSS THE MAP 45

GLOSSARY 46

FURTHER INFORMATION 47

INDEX 48

WHAT IS A DRAGON?

DRAGON BY ANOTHER NAME

Dragons are known around the world. The Chinese call them *lung*. Hawaiians say *kelekona*. They are *unktena* to the Cherokee and *smok* to the Polish. *Zmaj, tarakona, sarkany, tatsu, draig, lindorm, unhcegila, draak*. Wherever words have been spoken in the world, one is always reserved for the dragon.

Many cultures have depicted the dragon as a cross between a snake and a lizard with wings.

The common English word stems from the Greek *drakon*, meaning giant serpent or sea fish. Remarkably, every language's version of the word implies some kind of monstrous snake.

FAST FACT

The Persian word for dragon, *azhdaha*, describes a giant serpent that lives either on land or in the sea.

A GLOBAL AGREEMENT

It is remarkable that cultures around the world have similar ideas about what dragons are and what they look like. Most believe these monstrous serpents have two or four clawed feet. Dragons fly, with or without wings. Most cultures agree that they also spew fire or water.

Finally, most people agree that dragons are mythological. Myths are common beliefs rooted deep in the past. They are the stories that we tell to better understand the world around us — and ourselves.

Some cultures have myths about fighting dragons, while others worship them. It seems that these magical creatures have always fascinated humans.

While other mythical creatures come in many forms, cultures around the world share similar ideas about dragons.

SWOOP, SLITHER, SLASH

As far back as we can travel in time using **artifacts** and evidence, we can find mythical dragons. A 5,000 year-old Persian seal found in the Iranian city of Susa features the image of a dragon. A Sumerian hymn from 2500 BC honors the dragon sun god Ninurta. Similarly, the neighboring Babylonians told tales of Tiamat, the spirit of emptiness and chaos, who transformed into a dragon to battle another god.

Egyptian hieroglyphs from around 1300 BC include images of Great God, a winged snake with three heads and four clawed feet—a very recognizable dragon. Other Egyptian dragon-like deities include the goddess Mersokar and the god Chanuphis (or Bait).

Ancient Egyptians believed in a three-headed dragon.

The sky dragons in many Asian folktales were thought to spit lightning bolts!

UNSOLVED MYSTERIES

Long before these legends were pressed into metal or carved into stone, they existed as an oral tradition—stories memorized and repeated over many generations. Typically, these repetitions grew into myths because they explained natural events that people were not otherwise able to understand.

FAST FACT

Modern scientists still have not pinned down the exact cause for lightning, despite the aid of particle physics.

PROCEED WITH CAUTION

Myths can also serve as useful warnings. Prehistoric sightings of actual big snakes, such as pythons and boa constrictors, surely sparked tales warning people to avoid dangerous reptilian **habitats**. You would not want your friends or family to go near an African rock python, which can span 23 feet (7 m) and unhinge its jaws to swallow a whole gazelle! Likewise, encounters with Nile crocodiles were undoubtedly horrific, because they grow up to 16 feet long (5 m). The saltwater crocodile is even bigger, reaching 20 to 23 feet (6 to 7 m), maxing out at 2,600 pounds (1,179 kg)!

A Nile crocodile can weigh up to 1,600 pounds (725 kg). It is the second-largest reptile after the saltwater crocodile.

FAST FACT

One Inuit myth tells about the *kikituk*, a crocodilian dragon that came ashore to feast on people!

Discoveries of dinosaur fossils may have contributed to the belief that ferocious dragons roamed Earth.

MONSTROUS INSTINCTS

Puzzlingly, dragon myths survived in places where big snakes and monster crocodiles did not exist. Discoveries of dinosaur fossils by early civilizations may have inspired these fables. However, dragon tales persisted in places where no fossils have ever been unearthed. Could the stories have traveled along trade routes, carried by storytellers? Certainly, but that does not account for the fact that dragon stories have survived in even the remotest places—those cut off from all interaction with the outside world.

Somehow, people everywhere throughout time have known about dragons, as if by instinct.

TRIPLE THREAT

In the early 2000s, **anthropologist** David E. Jones noticed a strange coincidence. He found that nearly all monkey species have an instinctual fear of the same three predators: snakes, big cats, and birds of prey. Jones was an expert on human **evolution** and the development of cultures and civilizations.

To him, it made sense that **primates** would have a built-in fear of these particular predators because the earliest human ancestors battled them for millennia—some studies suggest as far back as 350 million years. The primates most likely to survive those battles would have passed on DNA—genetic programming—designed to avoid these predators' sinister slither, sharp teeth, or grasping talons.

Primates have had an instinctual fear of snakes, big cats, and birds of prey for millions of years.

The *pakhangba*, a dragon known in Manipur, India, has a crown of antlers and a body that is part lion and part snake.

FEAR FACTORS

Today, numerous studies of human behavior show a persistent, almost involuntary fear response to these traits. Babies are uncomfortable when shown two side-by-side black dots. Researchers speculate that the dots resemble the staring eyes of predators. Infants also display an almost **reflexive**, instinctual fear of snakes, cats, and birds that they don't feel for other animals. Also, many children develop intense phobias of these three creatures, whether or not they have ever encountered real, live specimens.

FAST FACT

The horns on many depictions of dragons can resemble cats' ears, which point backward like horns when cats prepare to attack. Also, the crowns of horns depicted on some dragons look a lot like ruffled feathers.

BODY OF EVIDENCE

The combined traits of snakes, cats, and raptors, jumbled together, have created the iconic image of the dragon that is known around the world. Ninurta, the dragon of the Sumerian hymn, has large, reptilian scales, forepaws like a lion's, and hind legs like an eagle's. The ancient Persian seal depicts a similar dragon, only with eagle talons up front. The Babylonians believed that Tiamat not only transformed into a serpent with a panther's forelegs, but could also summon an army of *sirrush*, which were mashed-up monsters. They were part raptor, part serpent, and part lion, with a dash of scorpion for bonus scary points.

This reconstructed image of a *sirrush* is displayed in the Istanbul Archaeological Museum in Istanbul, Turkey. The image, from the Ishtar Gate of the city of Babylon, dates back to the sixth century BC.

FAST FACT

A *sirrush* is a dragon with scales and a tongue like a snake's, eagle-like hind legs, catlike forelegs, and a long tail and neck.

TELLING TAILS

Across the expanse of ancient Chinese literature, from the oldest surviving text from 2700 BC to those produced in the Shang Dynasty (1600–1100 BC), there are descriptions of dragons with snake bodies, eagle claws, and cat fangs.

The Mongols, who raided the ancient regions of Asia, the Chukchi reindeer herders of Siberia, and the Olmec cultures of Central America all depicted dragons combining traits of big cats, raptors, and snakes. Olmec peoples included the Toltecs, Maya, and Aztecs.

SMAUG

Even Smaug—King Under the Mountain and dreaded dragon of J. R. R. Tolkien's fantasy classic *The Hobbit*—bears the combined predator traits in film adaptations of the book. Smaug has bat-like wings and talons. His body is that of a large serpent, but his face has the ragged jaws and angular nose of a snarling tiger. His tail swishes with feline pizzazz. Like Smaug, many other dragons are depicted with beards or tentacle-like growths around their faces, not unlike furry cat chins and whiskers.

This replica of Smaug the Golden was displayed in July 2014 at ComiCon in San Diego, California. Director Peter Jackson adapted *The Hobbit* into a trilogy of films (2012-2014).

TRICK OR BE A TREAT

To thwart the big birds, sneaky snakes, and creeping cats, human ancestors developed better survival strategies. They began to live in larger groups for protection—forming the first societies. They also developed elaborate calls to warn specifically against raptors, cats, and snakes—the first hints of language. Over long expanses of time, they outsmarted their predators. No longer subjected to constant threats, humans evolved and adopted the behaviors and activities that make them stand out in the animal kingdom. Religion, philosophy, and art became the prizes that human civilization won after defeating the **primordial** dragon. In some ways, the dragon myth has helped shape our existence.

This image of Tiamat and her *sirrush* army was discovered by an archeologist in 1899, who unearthed the Ishtar Gate. King Nebuchadnezzar II (605–562 BC) erected eight such gates as entrances into the great city of Babylon. This recreation stands in the Pergamon Museum in Berlin, Germany.

ON A SCALE OF GOOD TO BAD

A FEW BAD EGGS

Despite appearing more or less the same around the world, dragons do not behave uniformly. Most mythologies split down a clear line: either dragons are evil and harmful, or they are kind and helpful. The legend of Tiamat's dragon transformation might be seen as the parent of all "bad dragon" tales to follow. It establishes the dragon as a dangerous enemy, an opponent to fear and destroy.

BASILISK

The ancient Greeks and Romans feared the basilisk, a serpentine dragon with a hiss so frightful that all snakes fled from it. The spit of the basilisk was known to knock birds out of the sky. The ancient Greeks and Romans thought that the only way to kill the basilisk was by making it view its own terrible reflection in a mirror.

This brown basilisk is found in Mexico and Central and South America. It is also known as the Jesus Christ lizard because it can run across water.

LEGENDARY MONSTERS

In Scandinavian mythology, dragons were so dangerous that they threatened to undermine the very fabric of the universe. The world tree, Yggdrasil, held the universe together with its infinite branches and roots. But at the base of that tree prowled Nidhogg, or "Dread Biter," a dragon that chewed at the roots night after night.

SAINT GEORGE AND THE DRAGON

This view of the bad dragon persisted in the legend of Saint George, a Roman soldier who converted to Christianity in the sixth century AD. According to legend, George traveled far and wide, hoping to convert others to the new religion. In one town, he encountered a dragon, which he was certain was really the devil in disguise. George not only killed the dragon, but also convinced the townsfolk to adopt Christianity.

Saint George slays the dragon, shown here on this stained glass window.

BEWARE THE WORM

The *lindorm* was commonly depicted in central Europe. This dragon had a pair of arms that it used to dig up and devour dead bodies from graveyards. Wyverns, close cousins of the *lindorm*, were dragons with a pair of legs and a pair of wings. Wyverns were considered so ferocious that they became symbols of war across Britain and Europe. Kingdoms decorated their battle flags with wyverns. Soldiers painted them on their shields. Killing a brave leader in battle was called "slaying a dragon."

In parts of Germany, Austria, and Switzerland, old folktales warn about encountering the *tatzelwurm*. This dwarfish dragon measures only 4 to 5 feet (1.2 to 1.5 m) long, but it has sharp claws and a catlike head, and it delights in springing out of holes to snatch and eat passersby. In the forests around the Rhône River of France, people have been told for centuries to beware the *tarasque*. This half-fish, half-beast monster is said to gobble up travelers.

This statue of a *zilant*, another two-legged dragon, is located in Kazan, Russia. It is the official symbol of the city of Kazan.

FAST FACT
With only two legs, wyverns are easy to spot.

STRIKING SIMILARITIES

The early civilizations of North America also depicted dragons as fierce and dangerous creatures. Piasa was a dragon known among the ancient Mississippian cultures (AD 800–1600). Although the original murals are long gone from the limestone cliffs in present-day Illinois, sketches recorded in settlers' journals depict a fearsome bird with a scaly body, bat-like wings, bearded and horn-crowned cat head, and four eagle feet.

Painted by Native Americans, this reproduction of the original Piasa mural is located on the cliffs of the Mississippi River in Alton, Illinois, near the location of the original murals.

Where the Hiwassee and Valley Rivers meet in North Carolina, legends claimed there lived a leech-like dragon whose coiling body caused the waters to churn and foam. Get too close and the dragon might vomit foul liquid on you. Stunned, you'd fall into the raging waters and be swept downstream. Maybe your family would find your dead body washed ashore—nose and ears mysteriously sliced off.

FAST FACT

Ethiopian legends tell of a dragon with four wings and clawed feet. It feasted on elephants!

POWERFUL ALLIES

While some cultures feared the dragon, many others revered it. Anthropologists believe the dragon has always symbolized good qualities of strength, power, and wisdom in China. The most powerful families believed their lineages traced back to dragon ancestors. As a result, the robes of many emperors were adorned with a five-toed imperial dragon. During the Han period in China (206 BC–AD 220), the emperor's throne was the "dragon's seat," and his clothes were "dragon's robes."

For the Chinese, dragons have also embodied the awesome powers of nature. Shen-lung, the sky-dwelling dragon, was said to release Earth-rattling thunder when he roared, and he spewed rain on the thirsty crops and people below.

Today, Chinese dragons are often used to create light art.

WATER WORKS

Many dragons in Asia were worshiped because they seemed to rule over rivers, lakes, and the ocean. They were said to possess magical powers that influenced natural events, including rainfall, the tides, floods, and droughts. In India, a dragon named Vritra once held all the world's water.

The *o-gon-cho* dragon of Japan was believed to live at the bottom of a deep pond. When it howled, it signaled the coming of some disaster. Similarly, the native peoples of Australia tell tales of the Rainbow Serpent, a dragon that emerged from deep pools of water as bright, arching rainbows.

Nagas are ancient Indian dragons. This image depicts two nagas guarding a Buddhist temple.

FAST FACT

The Chinese dragon T'ao T'ieh was used as a friendly reminder not to overeat. His name meant "glutton," and he most certainly was one! He had a cavernous mouth and two hungry stomachs. T'ao T'ieh was painted on dinner plates to remind people not to stuff themselves too much.

This Mayan dragon sculpture is located at Chichén Itzá in Mexico.

DRAGONS OF DEVOTION

Friendly dragons have a history not only in Asia, but also in Europe and the Americas. The town of Klagenfurt, Austria, retains an elaborate dragon fountain inspired by the discovery of a *lindorm* skull in 1335. The skull was later proved to be a fossil from a woolly rhinoceros.

The Hopi, Zuni, and Keres tribes of North America worshiped the water serpent Pululukon. Central American civilizations admired amphipteres—legless, winged dragons. The Moki people of present-day Arizona worshiped Baho-li-kong-ya. This serpent-like dragon survives in artwork. It resembles a rattlesnake and it symbolizes fertility and the hope for new life.

Despite its violent plot, the Babylonian tale of Tiamat may also symbolize the same hope for new life. When the god Marduk defeated Tiamat, he sliced her serpent body in half. One portion became the sky and heaven, while the other transformed into the Earth. Her dragon blood created humankind.

HOW TO TAME YOUR DRAGON

Why were some dragons friendly, while others were not? Researchers and scholars are not entirely sure. One idea suggests that as governments or religions attempted to unite different tribes or clans under one authority, they cast the dragon as the supreme enemy. Heroes who set off to defeat the dragon **nemesis** were praised and beloved. Because they made the masses of people feel safe and protected, they were chosen to rule and given broad powers.

Scholars speculate that dragons were considered friendly in Asia because Asian empires were older than the kingdoms of Europe. As a result, people believed dragons had been tamed and made friendly long, long ago. Whatever the reason, dragon behaviors and habits have always managed to inspire our awe, challenge our beliefs, and drive our creative innovation.

This stained glass window located in Bayeux, France, shows Archangel Michael slaying a dragon that symbolizes Satan.

FAST FACT

Christianity demonized the dragon as the new religion grew from a small sect in the Roman Empire to a dominant world faith. Many of its early saints were also believed to be dragon slayers.

DRAGON BEHAVIOR

HATCHING HABITS

Whether a dragon is perceived as good or bad seems to have little impact on its basic behaviors. For example, dragons often guard something. The myth of guardian dragons may have come from an ancient vocabulary mixup! Like all homophones, the Ancient Greek words *drakon* and *draconta* might sound alike, but they have different meanings. One means "dragon," the other is "to watch or guard."

Dragons also tend to spray fire or water. Lastly, most cultures believe dragons fly, whether or not they have wings. Perhaps what is most surprising is how current scientific research has revealed each of these traits to be possible.

In most cultures, dragons were thought to have wings, breathe fire, and guard something of value.

FINDERS KEEPERS

One Chinese guardian dragon, Fu-ts'ang lung, stood watch over the world's deepest, darkest vaults filled with treasure, priceless jewels, and precious metals. Other dragons in Asian lore hoarded magic pearls in their mouths. In the Greek legend of Jason and the Argonauts, a dragon guards the Golden Fleece they seek. The Germanic tribes of Europe shared with the Norse traditions of Scandinavia a belief that dragons took up residence inside the burial mounds of great warriors, where they could be near gleaming heaps of treasure. And because water is a precious resource needed for life, many dragons guard it as if it were a prize.

The hero Beowulf slays many monsters, but dies of his wounds after battling a fire-breathing dragon.

A GRAVE REALIZATION

Beowulf is an Old English epic poem set in Scandinavia. In it, a dragon goes ballistic, spewing fire everywhere, when an item is stolen from the burial mound he has guarded for hundreds of years. The story may have some basis in science, because the mounds and tombs that dragons were said to guard built up flammable gases as the bodies and ritual offerings of food placed inside the mound rotted. A grave robber, like the one in *Beowulf*, could easily ignite the mound if he came by night, carrying a torch.

GROUNDED IN TRUTH

An understanding of geology might explain how natural and wondrous occurrences became ingredients in dragon myths. The soils of Northern Europe, where dragons are most often said to be fire-breathing, tend to be moist and dense. As a result, they trap pockets of flammable methane and hydrogen sulfide gases.

In the early days of mining for Earth's precious metals and jewels, excavators would have carried candles, torches, and other open flames to see while they dug deep tunnels. When their candles ignited pockets of gas, it must have seemed to the frantic miners that some fire-breathing monster was bent on keeping them away from the buried treasures.

Y Ddraig Goch, or the Red Dragon, has adorned the national flag of Wales for many centuries as a symbol of the country's power and the bravery of its people.

FAST FACT

The *tulihänd* was a small dragon from Estonia often employed to guard its master's treasure.

It's easy to see why people thought erupting volcanoes held fire-breathing dragons.

IGNITION SWITCH

Besides its association with igniting flammable gases, researchers think that the dragon's link with fire and treasures buried under mountains may connect to other natural occurrences that were also unexplained for much of human history. For instance, volcanoes might have appeared to be mountains with fire-belching dragons inside.

An absence of toothpaste may also have fueled the belief in fiery breath. Anyone who has ever caught a whiff of cat breath will easily understand how the part-cat dragons got a reputation for "breathing fire." Ornithologists—scientists who study birds—point out that raptors tend to have pretty foul breath, too, thanks to the rotten meat and bones digesting in their bellies.

SPITFIRE

Victims of a cobra strike might also find it easy to believe in fire-belching monsters. The cobra spits a toxic venom that can cause blisters and even blindness! In a fascinating twist of fact and fantasy, scientists hypothesize that dragons—had they really existed—might have developed flame glands the same way early snakes turned saliva glands into sacs of poisonous venom. Now add the fact that bacteria naturally present in most digestive organs produce highly flammable gaseous waste. Dragons could have employed these gut gases to spew fire. The friction of the gas against their teeth might have been enough to spark flames.

A REAL FIREFIGHTER

The bombardier beetle produces a toxic, flaming spray to ward off predators. When threatened, the bug churns up its own batch of hydrogen peroxide and hydroquinone. These chemicals mix in a sort of combustion chamber with reactive enzymes.

The bombardier beetle sprays a scalding "fire juice" from its hind end.

FAST FACT

Bombardier beetles are found on all continents around the globe except Antarctica.

A FOUNTAINHEAD

Besides fire, many dragons were believed to spew water. Vritra of ancient India released the world's water when he was killed and cut open. In the year AD 520, the people of Rouen, France (then the kingdom of Normandy) were said to suffer the arrival of a nightmarish dragon. It lurked in the Seine River, and it sprayed thousands of gallons of water across the lands, flooding fields and ruining crops. The people called it the *gargouille*, or "gargler." To this day, *gargouilles* can still be seen in France. Just look up at the gargoyles on the oldest churches and cathedrals!

The gargoyles of Notre Dame Cathedral in Paris are the most famous in the world. A spout inside each sculpture spews out the falling rain away from the building, preventing erosion of the walls.

One example of water-spewing occurring in nature involves the mighty and massive whale, which was once thought to be a dragon. Some whales, like the humpback, have blowholes that spray water. This spray can look like steam—water in its fiery form.

FLIGHT RISK

It's easy to understand why dragons were believed to fly, since these mythical beasts were most likely inspired by birds of prey. Scientists also think that dragons would have been good flyers if they existed in real life. Assuming they shared traits with the dinosaurs (who evolved into today's birds), dragons would have had hollow bones. Also, their scales might have aided their **aerodynamics**, just like the V-shaped scales on sharks help them slice through water.

Having hollow bones would mean that even a really big, blubbery dragon could fly because it would not weigh very much.

FAST FACT

The biggest bones in the world belong to a dinosaur species discovered in 2014. Members of the titanosaur family were basically five-story buildings on four legs, weighing in at 70 tons—or about the same weight as 14 African elephants.

Lizards of the **genus** *Draco*, also known as flying dragons, have a flap of skin that stretches like a fan and looks like wings. A flying lizard can glide from tree to tree for up to 150 feet (46 m).

WINGIN' IT

But what about dragons that could fly without wings, such as those common throughout Asian mythologies? In this case, observations of nature reveal a possible explanation. For example, flying snakes jump from tall trees, flatten their bodies like ribbons, and float over long distances. Some species of flying lizards do the same, using flaps of skin like parachutes. Ancient peoples might not have been able to explain aerodynamics, but they could easily have reasoned that even creatures without wings can fly.

FAST FACT

The Komodo dragon is the world's biggest lizard and the closest thing to a real dragon. It has a mouth full of 60 fangs, and saliva teeming with some 50 strains of deadly bacteria, so its bite is poisonous.

FIGHTING TOOTH AND CLAW

IN THE DRAGON'S LAIR

Dragons—both friendly or fierce—can be found everywhere today. They grapple with heroes in video games and role-playing games, such as the popular *Dungeons and Dragons*. They soar through the skies and terrorize victims in hit TV series such as *Merlin* and *Game of Thrones*. At various times, J.K. Rowling's hero, Harry Potter, escapes dragons' toothy attacks. Toothless, the loyal and cunning dragon in Cressida Cowell's *How to Train Your Dragon* stories, embodies all the best qualities of friendly, helpful dragons.

But how do the myths endure when science has managed to solve so many of the mysteries that created them? Why bother with dragons when the rise of civilization moved humanity out of the wilderness and into our safe, cozy homes where daily run-ins with raptors, snakes, and predatory cats are rare?

The balloon of Toothless the dragon is flown in New York City on November 28, 2013, at the Annual Macy's Thanksgiving Day Parade.

TEXT MESSAGES

One reason the myths endure might be that we continue to learn valuable lessons from dragons. Our earliest ancestors might have learned to recognize and run away from dragons by their characteristic swoop, slither, or slash. Indeed, the earliest dragons that slithered out of oral stories and onto the printed page were monsters. The *Epic of Gilgamesh*, thought to be the oldest surviving storybook in the world, mentions Humbaba, a fire-breathing, fanged dragon. The Roman hero Hercules killed the Hydra as one of 12 impossible tasks he was given. The Hydra was a multi-headed dragon that could swiftly regenerate new heads as soon as one was cut off.

LEVIATHAN

The Bible tells of Leviathan, a monstrous sea dragon, with 300 **incandescent** eyes. Leviathan was so large that it snacked on other dragons the way we crunch on popcorn.

According to legend, Leviathan breathed fire and was so huge that the sea boiled when he came to the surface.

BEHOLD, THE DRAGON SLAYER

Over time, humanity found other ways of dealing with the unknown. We discovered we could face our fears and stand our ground. To accomplish that, we invented the myth of the brave dragon slayer! The Greek god Zeus fought and destroyed Typhon, a demon dragon made up of many snakes, wings, and eyes that flashed fire. The hero Perseus took on Cetus, the serpent dragon that sea god Poseidon used like an attack dog. The Norse god Thor went on to slay Jörmungandr. And in another popular Norse legend, the boy Sigurd slayed the greedy, treasure-hoarding dragon, Fáfnir—once a man, cursed to live as a dragon.

This Greek stamp from 1973 shows Zeus fighting Typhon.

FAST FACT

Women dragon slayers are not as common in myths, but Saint Martha defeated the terrible *tarasque* of France. She tamed it and tied it up with her shawl. Actress Sigourney Weaver slayed slews of outer-space alien dragons in the *Alien* films. More recently, Emilia Clarke played the character Daenerys Targaryen, the amazing dragon mother in the TV series *Game of Thrones*.

WISE GUYS

Many ancient Chinese legends tell of heroes who, instead of slaying dragons, chose brains over brawn. For example, when a couple of trickster dragons made off with all the water in one region, the Ming Emperor sent the brave Gaoliang to hunt them down. Rather than shoot the dragons with his bow and arrow, Gaoliang targeted the dragon's enchanted clay pot and released all the stolen water. This enabled a great city to be built, which we now call Beijing.

WESTERN LEGENDS

For Western audiences, wicked dragons and their heroic slayers made the jump from oral storytelling to the written page. These characters thrived in the Arthurian legends and the many tales that imitated them. Dragons scurried and wriggled into fairy tales and operas. They fled the onslaught of heroes and made a home for themselves in comic books!

In medieval legends, knights fought dragons to save prisoners locked in castles.

FRIENDS AT LAST

Kenneth Grahame, a British author of children's fiction, introduced the West to its first popular friendly dragon when he published his story "The Reluctant Dragon" in 1898. Less than 50 years later, the Walt Disney Company—already a huge success in the film industry—turned the book into a hit cartoon. Disney went on to create other memorable and friendly dragons, such as Elliott in *Pete's Dragon*, and Mushu, the quick-witted sidekick in *Mulan*. Similarly, in Japanese animation, Hayao Miyazaki's 2001 animated film *Spirited Away* starred a shape-shifting dragon named Haku, who does all he can to help young Chihiro save her parents from a wicked curse.

This dragon statue from Tehran, Iran, is an example of the friendly dragons known throughout Asia and the Middle East.

FLIGHTS OF FANCY

Dragons experienced only a brief struggle while clawing their way into motion pictures. Poor special effects risked turning the fiercest dragon into a laughing stock. Luckily, the special effects in the 1922–24 two-part movie, *The Niebelungs,* did a decent job bringing to life a frightful Fáfnir. Budding attempts to mix live action and animation enabled Sinbad to battle a dragon in the 1958 movie *The Seventh Voyage of Sinbad.*

Clearly, dragons prove to be a durable, global, and somewhat immortal myth. Now, they are ready to teach us the most crucial lesson about survival.

FALKOR

In the early 1980s, *The Neverending Story* featured a truly believable live-action dragon named Falkor. Falkor was a technological feat. The puppet measured 43 feet (13 m) long and used the latest in animatronics (intricate robotics) and computer-generated imagery, or CGI. At the time, CGI was still very new. Now, it is an essential element in the movie magic of special effects.

In 2008, fans in Portugal recreated a life-sized sand sculpture honoring the beloved dragon Falkor.

EVADING EXTINCTION

LOCH NESS UNLOCKED

In September, 2016, Ian Bremner of Scotland was out for his usual weekend adventures, snapping scenic nature photographs. He stopped along the shores of Loch Ness. His camera clicked away, recording shot after shot of the sun flickering off the dark waters. Then suddenly, there it was—a long, silvery, serpentine creature ripping across the channel!

Many who saw the crisp photograph plastered across news sites claimed that Bremner had finally captured the first, definitive proof that the legendary Loch Ness Monster existed. Others saw only a line of seals diving into the water.

This illustration shows what some people think the Loch Ness Monster, or Nessie, may look like.

FAST FACT

Over 1,000 people have claimed to have seen the Loch Ness Monster.

According to legend, the ogopogo haunts the waters of Okanagan Lake in Canada.

FATHOM THAT

Similar sea beast sightings still come out of Norway, Japan, and Canada. Witnesses describe dragon-like creatures emerging from the waters of Papua New Guinea's Lake Dakataua and Flathead Lake in the United States. The descriptions are so strikingly similar that some scientists wondered if the creature might be some deep-water descendent of the *basilosaurus*, a giant whale that roamed Earth's oceans long ago. After all, the monster captured in grainy pictures and film footage swims as a *basilosaurus* would, by arching its long body into a vertical sort of slither. On land or water, modern snakes slither from side to side. Nonetheless, plenty of other researchers don't agree because the *basilosaurus* became **extinct** some 25 million years ago!

If dragons aren't real and dinosaurs really are extinct, then how do we account for sightings of dragon-like creatures such as the Loch Ness Monster?

MASS DELUSIONS

How can we account for these widespread sightings of mythical beasts? The human brain adapts readily to suggestion and expectation. You can test this ability by using reversible optical illusion images such as the ones on this page. Ask your friends what they see and you are likely to get different answers. Select a second group of friends and ask them if they see the duck and the goblet. Odds are good they will see exactly what you told them to see. Your suggestion prompted their brains to ignore other possibilities.

The same effect is true for Ian Bremner's Loch Ness Monster photograph. Tell people it features an ancient sea beast, and that is what they will see. Or tell them it shows three seals, and they will never even imagine a monster.

Our ability to "see" dragons rests in the brain's ability to reinterpret information, like this reversible image. What do you see – a goblet or two faces; a duck or a rabbit? Or something else entirely?

INFECTIOUS IDEAS

Human history is full of these illusions. When the deceptions affect large populations, they are known as mass delusions or mass hysterias. For example, in 1518, a dance-attack struck the residents of Strasbourg, France. People inexplicably began dancing without rest for days on end. Many died from heart attacks or exhaustion. Similarly, a girl's school in Kashasha, Tanzania, in Africa suffered a severe laughing epidemic in 1962. When the school had to shut down, the girls were sent home, where their giggle epidemic spread to neighboring villages and schools.

BEWITCHING BEHAVIOR

Perhaps one of the most famous mass delusions took place in Salem, Massachusetts. In the cold months early in 1692, numerous girls suffered from strange fits and outbursts. Their symptoms spread to other girls. When concerned adults suspected witchcraft, the girls made quick accusations. Pretty soon, everyone in Salem claimed to have seen a neighbor or acquaintance perform some spectacular bit of black magic.

Following the Salem witch trials, at least 20 so-called witches were tried and executed.

DISORDERLY CONDUCT

Other hysterias have occurred more recently in places including Mexico City, New York, the state of Virginia, and Afghanistan and Malaysia. Doctors and psychiatrists believed that victims turned their stress or fears into physical illnesses, such as shaking, seizures, or a rash. The condition spreads because that is what we expect diseases to do!

Suggestion may have played a large and powerful part in the eyewitness testimonies of many dragon sightings. Some people "saw" an imaginary monster in the waters of Loch Ness because they expected to see it.

GREAT GALACTIC GHOUL

NASA astronauts whisper about the Great Galactic Ghoul, a sort of Loch Ness Monster in space. It causes spacecraft to disappear mysteriously, and no one knows why. The Great Galactic Ghoul has been blamed for many of these failures.

More than half of the spacecraft launched toward Mars have failed. Some people believe that the Great Galactic Ghoul devours these vessels!

LOST WORLD

Whether or not we truly see real dragons today, one thing is certain: we think of them differently today than we did thousands of years ago. In many ways, the dragons popular in our books and movies remind us that the world isn't what it once was.

In 4.6 billion years, the planet has undergone **cataclysmic** changes. Oceans swelled and glaciers spread. Volcanoes spewed and earthquakes swallowed mountain ranges. Life-forms on this planet have also come and gone.

FAST FACT

Long ago, it's said that Sir John of the Thumbs drove the last dragon out of Denbigh, Wales. Sir John had two thumbs on each hand, much like koalas. He showed these to the dragon, who was too distracted and befuddled to fight back. In Welsh, *denbigh* or *dim-bych* means "no more dragon."

Scientists have found evidence of at least five mass extinctions, or episodes when more than half of all species died in a short span of several million years.

In some Chinese and Japanese myths, dragons transform into pine trees, which still display the dragons' rough scales in their bark.

DESTRUCTIVE POWERS

About 65 million years ago, an asteroid measuring 6 miles (10 km) long shot the Earth like a bullet and kicked off a mass extinction of dinosaurs and plant life. Today, some scientists think that over half the world's animal and plant species will die off due to human destruction or alteration of the planet.

This profound silencing of life on Earth echoes in many of today's dragon tales. Dragons are often portrayed as the last of their kind, or a dying species. If they are violent, it is because they must fight for their survival.

DARING THE DRAGON

In many ways, by shifting our view of dragons, we have shifted how we see ourselves. Once, we were hapless prey—defenseless, tree-dwelling mammals and the favorite snack of deadly serpents, raptors, and jungle cats. We may have survived and thrived partly because we converted our enemies into a single, monstrous myth. We tamed the beast, and with it, the world.

Now, we humans no longer see ourselves as victims, but masters of the universe. Yet we also see who the real victims are: dragons, along with so many other animals, going the way of the dinosaur. In a world full of so much danger and disagreement, what new modes of survival will we uncover if we dare to keep learning what the dragon myths have to teach us?

Inside Beijing's Beihai Park stands one of three Nine-Dragon Walls – considered the most beautiful of all such walls. Built in the 1700s, this wall stands almost 50 feet (15 m) high, extending nearly 70 feet (21 m) long. It displays nine magnificent dragons and 626 smaller dragons.

DRAGON MYTHS ACROSS THE MAP

Here are some of the places where dragon myths originated.

MAP KEY

1. Australia
2. Austria
3. Canada
4. China
5. Denmark
6. Egypt
7. England
8. Ethiopia
9. France
10. Germany
11. Greece
12. Guatemala
13. Hawaii
14. Hollywood
15. Iceland
16. India
17. Iran
18. Iraq
19. Ireland
20. Italy
21. Japan
22. Komodo Island
23. Mexico
24. Mongolia
25. Norway
26. Papua New Guinea
27. Poland
28. Russia
29. Scotland
30. Sweden
31. Switzerland
32. Tanzania
33. United States
34. Wales

GLOSSARY

aerodynamics a science that deals with the motion of gaseous fluids (such as air) and with the forces acting on bodies exposed to them

anthropologist a scientist who studies humans and their cultures

artifact a cultural or historical object made by a human

cataclysmic a sudden, violent upheaval

evolution the process by which living organisms develop over time

extinct no longer existing

genus a biological category that contains related species

habitat the natural home of a living plant or animal

incandescent glowing with bright light or great heat

nemesis an inescapable rival or opponent

primate a category of mammal that has hands and feet that grasp and that includes humans, apes, monkeys, and lemurs

primordial existing since the beginning of time

reflexive behavior that occurs automatically without thinking

FURTHER INFORMATION

BOOKS

McCullough, Joseph A. *Dragonslayers: From Beowulf to St. George*. Osprey Publishing, 2013.

Norell, Mark A. and Kendall, Laurel. *Mythic Creatures: And the Impossibly Real Animals Who Inspired Them*. New York: Sterling Signature, 2016.

Paolini, Christopher. *The Inheritance Cycle*. New York: Knopf, 2012.

WEBSITES

Meet five dragons from around the world here!
https://www.dkfindout.com/us/explore/how-to-spot-dragon-five-dragons-from-around-world/

Learn about real-life dragons at this awesome site.
https://nationalzoo.si.edu/animals/komodo-dragon

Learn more about real animals that could have inspired dragon myths!
http://www.smithsonianmag.com/science-nature/where-did-dragons-come-from-23969126/

INDEX

Archangel Michael, 22
Beowulf (poem), 24
birds, 10, 11, 14, 15, 18, 26, 29
Bremner, Ian, 37, 39
cats, 10, 11, 12, 13, 14, 17, 18, 26, 44
Clarke, Emilia, 33
Cowell, Cressida, 31
delusions, 39, 40
demons, 22, 33
dinosaur, 9, 29, 38, 43
Dungeons & Dragons (game), 31
evolution, 10, 29
extinction, 37, 38, 42, 43
fire, 5, 23, 24, 25, 26, 27, 28, 32, 33
flight, 5, 23, 29, 30
fossils, 9, 21
Game of Thrones, 31, 33
Gilgamesh, Epic of, 32
Grahame, Kenneth, 35
Great Galactic Ghoul, 41
guardians, 20, 23, 24, 25
How to Train Your Dragon, 31
hysteria, 40, 41
Jackson, Peter, 13
Jason and the Argonauts, 24
Jones, David E., 10
Leviathan, 32
lindorm, 4, 17, 21
Loch Ness Monster (Nessie), 37, 38, 39, 41
magic, 20, 24, 36, 40
Miyazaki, Hayao, 35
Mulan (film), 35
National Aeronautics and Space Administration (NASA), 41
Neverending Story, The (film), 36
Niebelungs, The (film), 35
Pete's Dragon (film), 35
raptors, 12, 13, 14, 26, 31, 44
Red Dragon, 25
"Reluctant Dragon, The" (story), 35
reptiles, 8, 12, 29
Rowling, J.K., 31
Saint George, 16
Saint Martha, 33
serpents, 12, 13, 15, 20, 33, 37, 44
Seventh Voyage of Sinbad, The (film), 35
Sir John of the Thumbs, 42
snakes, 4, 6, 8, 9, 10, 11, 12, 13, 14, 15, 21, 27, 30, 31, 33, 38
Spirited Away (film), 35
Tiamat, 6, 12, 14, 15, 21
Tolkien, J. R. R., 13
treasure, 24, 25, 26, 33
volcanoes, 26, 42
Walt Disney Company, 35
Weaver, Sigorney, 33